Essentials for
CIVIL DIALOGUE

MARK FOSDAL

Copyright © 2020 by Mark Fosdal

All rights reserved. No part of this book may be reproduced or used in any manner without permission of the copyright owner.
mark.fosdal@gmail.com

First paperback edition September 2020
Cover and design by B. Spears
Illustrations by J. Nazarova
Photography R. Winkle
Edited by L. Booth

ISBN – 978-0-578-78211-9 (6.5x6.5 IngramSpark paperback)

To my family

Eating together,
With civility among
All generations.

CONTENTS

Section One: Insights for Civil Dialogue   1

Section Two: Insights for Diverse Ideologies   75

Section Three: Topics for Discussion   133

Acknowledgments

Special gratitude extended to those in my political discussion groups and social circles, to my corporate colleagues, and to those concerned parents who patiently conversed with me as I learned about your perspectives. I hope these insights improve the quality of your discussions with your loved ones and neighbors.

We are a nation having witnessed moments of triumph and civil unrest when striving to establish equality for all. Ingrained in our culture is the story of redemption with our proudest moments being achieved through civil discussions between those having diverse perspectives. *Therefore*, let us remind ourselves of our common identity as we accept personal accountability to create a healthier nation and a better world through civil dialogue.

With Sincerest Regards,

Mark Fosdal

Only time with someone can cultivate a relationship in which perspectives change.

Section One:
INSIGHTS FOR CIVIL DIALOGUE

There is mounting frustration for those desiring to have good discussions. It takes practice to have a conversation where the goal is to build or enhance a relationship when discussing sensitive topics. This type of conversation may feel counter-intuitive as we struggle to keep an open mind as we innately desire to persuade others rather than understand them.

Having such discussions is challenging as our opinion may reveal part of our core values. When someone disagrees with our opinion or treats us disrespectfully, it can be perceived as a personal attack on our values or identity. We may respond by withdrawing from the discussion or passively agree as we attempt to transition topics.

In order to avoid such situations, taking the time to better understand which values or part of our life experiences are associated with a political topic can help identify our bias as well as mitigate the emotional toll it may have as we begin to share our point of view. For example, by first understanding our personal experiences of becoming a citizen, being of an ethnic minority group, or a person of faith aids in detecting our bias and can certainly mitigate some of the emotional triggers when topics related to our life story are discussed.

The following insights were created to encourage personal reflection or facilitate a conversation with others that empowers us to understand our story and improve our ability to have a fruitful discussion. They were created by observing a variety of dynamics portrayed in our social circles, the media, and those in the public's eye as we struggle to integrate civility while expressing our opinions. When reviewing the insights, write down some personal memories, thoughts, or areas where there is room for improvement. *The more we understand how our story is associated with our viewpoints, the more likely we will be able to maintain a temperament that is conducive for an enlightening conversation and understand the dynamics of the group.*

- Which insights do you disagree with?
- Which insights reflect core values?
- Which insights can you relate to from past conversations?
- Which insights are most important to teach our youth?
- Can you identify role models that portray healthy dialogue?

Critical thinking involves expanding our knowledge to the particulars of a situation, using wisdom to discern the right path forward, and executing the plan in a disciplined manner. Embracing such attributes do not occur by chance, but through vision and determination.

Ask questions and listen. Listening is not a sign of submission, agreement, or passivity but a sign of respect.

The goal of a civil discussion is to understand,
not to persuade. Tempers flare when
there are unrealistic expectations.
Minds can change over time.

We have three types of stories that help form our identities: those we live with every day, those we choose to set aside, and those from our past. Understanding our story reveals our bias; integrating our story with opinions provides context and understanding.

Incorporating one's story is essential with any exchange. Set aside at least 30 minutes to begin a healthy discussion. This allows understanding to coexist with disagreement.

When you feel offended, it may be that someone has challenged your core beliefs; stay engaged, and inquire further.

Lowering your sense of entitlement will reduce your frustration during conversations. This form of humility creates an atmosphere of respect and productive engagement.

Resist the desire to sound important, and verify information before reposting on social media. Exercising your freedom in spreading misinformation is costly to all.

Stay curious. You can always learn something.

Show grace when receiving an improper comment due to others' triggered emotions or naïve understanding. This will create a safe environment for others to share opinions freely.

Be sure to understand before you disagree. We have an affinity for engaging with those who prioritize understanding while still being able to respectfully disagree.

If you are confused about someone's intensity, inquire about their story. It may add clarity to their frustration and enhance the discussion.

Condemning an action is appropriate, but use caution when condemning a person with a different ideology. This type of judgment generates fear and shame, which impairs intelligent discussion.

If people are offended by your viewpoint, reassess your tone or body language, and consider improving your communication style. If they continue to be offended, politely move on to another topic.

Limit your time in social circles
where rude behavior is the norm.
You will learn their bad habits faster
than teaching them healthy ones.

Being concise with your opinion is appreciated by all. This discipline stems from forethought and generates respect from your peers.

Communicating with frustration or anger is counterproductive. You're requiring your audience to navigate your emotions while responding to your perspective. With that said, passion is important.

Be transparent when someone has triggered a strong reaction with a comment. This allows you to talk through your emotions while still making your point.

Evaluate the importance of any affiliations before discussing politics. Maintaining healthy work or family relationships might take priority.

The message of "love your neighbor" has been diluted to a slogan of liking those you agree with. Instead, practice hospitality, which essentially means to embrace a stranger.

Avoid using ambiguous terms or slogans, as it leaves your ideas open to interpretation and propagates confusion when people refute your position.

Engage with people of different ideologies in the same manner wine connoisseurs expand their palate. With an open mind, they identify characteristics that make each wine unique.

Having bias is a human trait, not a character flaw. However, failing to recognize your bias results in false bravado and a habit of reviewing media that only reaffirms your views, thus reducing curiosity.

Speaking with discernment, the healthy form
of judgment, is the solution for those
struggling with passivity or fear of
offending others. More than ever,
we need those with life experience
to share their wisdom.

Verbalize commonalities, as we tend to gravitate toward our differences. Sharing mutual interests provides the foundation for exploring solutions.

Discussion over food and wine has worked for millennia. Only time with someone can cultivate a relationship in which perspectives change.

Publicly disagreeing with those of similar ideologies shows an identity rooted in the common good for all. Trust develops when impartiality is observed.

We reveal part of our identity when expressing opinions, making us feel more vulnerable. Therefore, approach each other with respect.

Permit yourself to make mistakes when expressing a viewpoint. It is a learning process that needs practice.

Do your best to use appropriate vocabulary, but avoid situations that are too oriented toward political correctness. It can destabilize the dynamic of the discussion.

Using only statistics to support your view puts you at risk for being used to advance the media's narrative. Make every attempt to check the primary source of data, and remember the human element behind the numbers.

Referencing only stories from the news to support your view also puts you at risk for being used to advance the media's narrative. Make the effort to see if the story reflects regional and national trends.

Take an internal assessment of your emotional well-being before a discussion. Those tired of explaining themselves should rest.

Instead of telling people *what* to think, show them *how* to think. Lead by example in assessing your bias, asking intelligent questions, and showing respect. Solutions will evolve over time with critical thinking.

Even when citing incorrect information, we can persuade people with our tone and body language. Since few of us are content experts, share opinions with humility.

Speak up when basic rights are threatened, independent of their ideology. It sends a strong message to our children that people take priority over politics.

Critical thinking is being meticulous in formulating questions. Poor questions lead to repetitive debates without solutions. Accurate observation, recognizing bias and researching primary sources are healthy traits needed to articulate good questions.

Civil discourse along a spectrum of ideologies are the cornerstone to any democratic republic. Our forefathers planned for factions to be held in check through such discussion.

When listening to the news, avoid both fatalistic and imperialistic viewpoints. The truth likely lies somewhere in between.

Know the difference between your beliefs and opinions. It will save time and energy when defending your beliefs while still being open to changing your opinions.

Fear plays a role in forming opinions.
By avoiding fear as a tactic and
acknowledging another's fear during a
discussion, ignorance is replaced
with trust and solutions are found.

There is no reason to make inflammatory statements about Christians on Easter, Muslims during Ramadan, or the military on Memorial Day. You gain respect and credibility with your opinion by honoring the traditions of others.

Maybe Twitter should encourage the use
of haikus to challenge our intellect
and dampen our temperament.

Regretting previously held viewpoints is understandable. However, avoid those who shame you into silence for past opinions. We need role models that have the integrity to publicly share their stories of growth.

A clear message should communicate the same meaning to everyone. Avoid being so diplomatic that your opinion is diluted to non-offensive gibberish.

Never before have we had so much exposure to the masses through our media with so little to say. During the civil rights movement, advocates fought vigorously to gain the media's attention to share their message of reform. Use your platform wisely.

Attempt to stay informed with current events using diverse media sources as you would seek a well-balanced diet at a convenience store. Options may be limited, but do the best you can.

Avoid answering questions when you disagree with the premise. Any reply is seen as consent to the premise, and your response will likely be taken out of context.

History suggests we connect personally when grudges develop while avoiding theatrics through the media. Adams and Jefferson settled their differences with respectful dialogue via personal letters. Burr and Hamilton argued their differences in the public forum, eventually leading to the death of Hamilton in a duel.

A successful life is finding the cadence between your identity and purpose. A common purpose we share is speaking up for the marginalized, independent of their ideology.

Our innate desire to please others predisposes us to participate in mob rule or to rationalize our silence in order to appease those nearby. Pleasing people is not the means to personal happiness and hinders good policy.

Some people won't like you if they can't
control you. This type of manipulation
is a common form of persuasion.
Guard yourself from this type of influence.

Avoid explaining your opinion to those not listening. Such situations usually create a combative atmosphere where needless resentment builds. Your actions of civility will suffice.

Temperament is to dialogue as breathing is to yoga. Both require a disciplined mind in remembering the fundamentals.

Asking rhetorical questions confuses your audience and can be interpreted as passive-aggressive behavior; instead, state your opinion, and ask for feedback.

Using derogatory terms reduces your credibility. It reveals a poor temperament and an opinion that has not been thought through.

Embrace the awkwardness of healthy dialogue. It is a blend of group therapy and public speaking for a society that has become lazy with genuine engagement.

When debating ideas, assume your opponent's motives are pure. After rapport has been developed, assess motives with questions instead of making accusations.

A genuine apology leads to changed behavior and transforms the cultural norm. Attempted reform based on sheer will power leads to frustration as repetitious behavior ensues.

It is more important to be understood than to sound intelligent. Know your audience, and communicate at their level.

Changing topics in the middle of a debate creates the same confusion with participants as saying UNO during a poker tournament. Please practice structured reasoning so that others can follow your rationale.

Do not be discouraged if you cannot
completely understand a person's journey.
Empathy begins by using your
story to relate to their circumstance.

The goal of anarchy is to remove law, whereas the goal of civil discussion is appealing to the rule of law.

Assert yourself, and reorient others to your identity if being labeled as leaning left or right. Your story as a parent, person of faith or an environmentalist may be more appropriate in branding your identity than the label society wants gives you.

When somebody asks if you prefer
thyme or oregano, feel free to say salt.

Forgiveness is the first step toward reconciliation. Gossip, a grudge, or ill will toward another hinder progress. With that said, reconciliation can only occur when there is a safe environment, and requires intent from the involved parties.

Being liked, agreed with and respected are not one in the same. Create space where respect and disagreement can co-exist and being liked is secondary.

Avoid situations where you are requested to respond to questions in a certain format or if you cannot ask follow-up questions. They are likely protecting a fragile concept without having viable solutions.

When a respectful relationship exists, a little humor can keep the conversation light when discussing politics.

Expand your political palate in the same manner wine connoisseurs explore a variety of wines.

Section Two:

INSIGHTS FOR DIVERSE IDEOLOGIES

Whether our national division has been present for decades or appeared more recently, there is little debate that social media has created a medium where not-so-subtle narratives are communicated from a variety of ideologies with varying degrees of civility. As our society has mimicked such rhetoric, it's common to end a discussion still confused about the other's opinion, not having completely identified the essential concepts interwoven into their spoken viewpoint. For example, underlying power struggles, the concept of a universal truth, or where accountability resides are just a few principles that may not be directly expressed during a discussion but are underlying themes to several different opinions. By understanding central differences between ideologies, we are better equipped to ask relevant questions and experience a more engaging conversation.

This next selection of insights will expand our "political palate" as we embrace different ideologies with the same curiosity as we would if attending a wine tasting event. Keeping an open mind during a discussion, asking clarifying questions to understand nuances is a sign of respect as well as the means by which we can expand our knowledge.

We develop a deeper understanding of our own opinion and how we process information as we interact with those of opposing viewpoints.

The following insights span diverse ideologies integrated within people's opinions but may not be overtly mentioned during a discussion. These are meant to evoke memories and emotions from previous encounters which may have elicited some disagreement or confusion. Take some time for self-reflection in writing down some thoughts when answering the following questions.

- Which insights elicits anger, fear or frustration?
- What specific measures can you take to mitigate such emotions in order to have a conversation with those of different ideologies?
- What specific points would you make about an insight during a discussion?
- Which insights aid in clarifying your core beliefs?
- What overriding themes do you agree or disagree with?
- Which principles would you emphasize to our youth as critical for making decisions on policy?
- Which public figures or policies come to mind with an insight?

The effects of racism are multiplied by people and institutions of power. Creating awareness, accountability, and a path for justice are the first steps to reconciliation.

Our federal republic may not endure if capitalism places compassion secondary to fiduciary responsibility. Democracy, in any form, has never flourished when intercession on behalf of the marginalized is ignored.

Striving for equality should not evolve into retribution. Welcome accountability from all parties when seeking the right balance in creating new policy.

Subtle racism is the fertilizer for overt hatred and requires a paradigm shift in our culture of understanding and dialogue. Remaining alert to oneself and the immediate environment is the first step on the road to reform.

The best solutions involve personal accountability and send a message that you are invested in working together for our mutual interests.

Making a statement through actions can be more effective than words. In time, words may be necessary, while your actions of civility will have provided any needed credibility.

Creating law without integrating the value of caring for the marginalized is as precarious as building a brick wall without mortar. It will never withstand time, no matter how solid the foundation.

There is truth; search for it, and protect it.
Without truth, we can rationalize injustice
during any era, as the end justifies the means.

Those born with multiple factors predisposing
them to be marginalized are the most vulnerable
in a system created to keep power with white
individuals. This necessitates systemic
changes in laws and our culture
to steer us in the direction of equality.

A politician's behavior reflects his or her legacy; how you respond reflects yours. Focus your energy on things you can change instead of grumbling.

A community can live in harmony when they have a shared identity. Actively search for fundamental similarities with your neighbors to build alliances.

Decisions made from anger or frustration have chaotic outcomes. Develop a disciplined approach to critical thinking while finding allies to further your cause.

We should hold a foreign government
accountable for poor policies while
remaining civil to those sharing its heritage.
Disregarding either leads to turmoil.

Advocating for the rights of a few at the expense of the majority is an ethical dilemma. Approach factions astutely, while balancing individual liberty with the common good for all.

As our changing laws reflect an evolving republic, it would be irresponsible to assume our values remain steadfast. Reinforce core values with your family and community while questioning authority.

Greed is a flaw of the heart, not of the pocketbook. Acknowledging this allows reform in closing loopholes for the wealthy while also detecting fraud in our welfare system.

Pride always competes, always divides, and is easier to see in someone else. This human trait may be most responsible for creating division within society.

Declaring God is on your side is as ludicrous as declaring the sun reflects light from the moon. In observing your apathy, people are repulsed by your God or religion when hypocrisy and injustice persist.

It is disrespectful to relabel an opposing viewpoint to be the antithesis of your own and analogous to the Yankees renaming the Red Sox to the Anti-Yankees. Out of respect, let others represent their viewpoint.

Exercising our freedom without responsibility leads to chaos. Acting with selfish intentions in the name of liberty breeds rival factions resulting in political, financial, civil, and moral unrest.

Effective politicians create a team that adapts to change. Avoid referring to their decisions as mistakes when the facts are still rolling in. True mistakes occur when bias clouds judgment or decisions are made in haste and left unchallenged.

Raising awareness to only one dimension of a complex social issue reflects a loss of objectivity. To maintain credibility, verbalize any potential inherent bias that may exist and welcome feedback.

Be quick to forgive, and gain assurance from changed behavior, as it endures not from a sense of obligation or guilt but from a transformed heart of compassion with new understanding.

Tolerance as a goal without engagement leads to subtle division. This type of tolerance is the default mode between people of different ideologies and gives a false sense of security that all is well in society.

Tolerance of different ideologies is the fruit of respectful engagement when showing hospitality. This creates a solid foundation for living through turbulent times.

The perception of power drives many discussions: who has it, who abuses it, and who needs it. Identifying this fundamental ideology early reorients the discussion and avoids frivolous debate over transient topics.

Be proud of your journey but do not be prideful. Pride will reduce your desire to mentor others as well as isolate you from allies to further a cause.

Proclaiming that the origin of a problem is beyond your control propagates helplessness and frustration. Collaborate where you can make a difference to empower those feeling marginalized.

Having shared values with a politician is an appropriate litmus test for identifying effective leadership. Sound character withstands hardship and inspires others to follow.

An effective politician may not be a popular leader. Remaining steadfast for the common good will create friction with various factions.

When there is injustice, harnessing righteous anger can lead to change. This type of anger brings people together for a common cause while avoiding destructive behavior.

Using non-violence is the preferred means to promote the need for change. If leadership remains apathetic, allowing more aggressive forms of protesting is justified to attain justice.

Momentum begins by implementing local solutions to local problems. Acquaint yourself with local politicians, and avoid the lure of the mainstream media's spotlight on national debates as the only means for change.

Platforms using ambiguous terminology always lead to more division. Seek clarity to the problem in order to assess for viable solutions.

Advancing personal agendas by misrepresenting current events can tarnish worthy platforms. Consider the implications to those affected by your lies.

Do not compete to see who has had more barriers in life. You are missing the point and isolating yourself from allies. Set aside this type of pride, and work together for common goals.

Apathy toward diverse ethnicities cultivates racism. Stay engaged with people of color having common interests, and remain observant.

The breakdown of the nuclear family is the primary reason for the disintegration of cultural norms. Ignoring this fundamental cause diverts any true reform.

Activism without raising awareness results in apathy. Activism without executing a plan leads to repetition.

Be alert for complacency when advocating any social justice platform. Your action is not meant to relieve your perceived guilt but to further a cause beyond yourself.

Yielding positions of power to those otherwise marginalized should be encouraged. Take practical steps in your life to empower others for leadership roles.

Unjust laws have ramifications for decades with consequences seen in our penal system, resulting in broken families and financial hardships. Compensation instead of a mere apology is the true sign of reconciliation.

Indoctrinating students of color with misleading narratives has created a generation of young adults confused about their identity. Providing culturally appropriate materials and a deeper appreciation for self-accountability can empower the next generation.

At the very least, people of faith should be aware of society's apathy in serving the marginalized and take action without adding to our division over trivial matters.

Showing support for an entity despite its flaws is necessary and appreciated. It reinforces a core value of not abandoning institutions during trials, and the antithesis to our cancel culture.

Kneeling during the national anthem may signify a heavy heart struggling in the moment rather than rebellion or disrespect. Yearn for the day we can stand together.

Our society has evolved over the decades with
like-minded people gathering together,
luring us deeper into a state of apathy.
Engage with those of different ideologies.

Becoming aware of privileges requires diligence. Blaming the marginalized individual or referencing the bootstrap theory are socially acceptable versions of covert white supremacy and should be discouraged.

The goal for some factions is to divide our country by removing fundamental pillars that provide security. Ask questions while looking for destructive patterns with their intent, and support reform when achievable goals are possible.

Before feeling repulsed upon hearing that you might exhibit racist behavior, take an internal assessment of what bias you may have toward those of different cultures and how it has formed your impression of them.

Our most prized and greatest obligation
is the education of our children. It would be
a grave disservice to our future if we did
not reveal with brutal honestly the
historical periods of racial discrimination.

Systemic apathy toward mental wellness propagates homelessness, drug abuse, and violence. It's systemic because we minimize the problem while limiting solutions pertaining to public education and lobbying power.

I'm not judging, but think your idea is
missing a couple of stickers on the Rubik's Cube.
Just sayin'.

Embrace the awkwardness of healthy dialogue. It is a blend of group therapy and public speaking for a society that has become lazy with genuine engagement.

Section Three:
TOPICS FOR DISCUSSION

After attaining a general understanding of the essentials for civil discussion and the range of diverse perspectives, we can begin to have a more focused dialogue about topics that resonate with us. Creating a culture where people feel safe sharing their opinion is paramount. Several online forums or local organizations have created such venues for curious people to engage in healthy discussions. Beginning such discussions with strangers reduces the likelihood of past dynamics being reinforced during a discussion (once a middle child, always a middle child) or tarnish present relationships essential in our daily life.

As we develop a method of critical thinking with our approach to topics and the desire to learn from others, we can create more intimate settings for in-person discussions if desirable. Over time, anger from past discussions dissipates and newer understanding replaces ignorance and fear. In situations where maintaining relationships with family or employees are a priority, acting with civility while verbalizing healthy boundaries seems to be the best approach.

Eventually we develop a deeper respect for others who we may have once despised. Genuine concern for their well-being, or group activities with shared interests are natural products of genuine engagement. This is the healthiest form of tolerance as a natural byproduct of genuine engagement where respect and disagreement can co-exist.

The following section contains polarizing statements to facilitate dialogue with people having different perspectives. While applying insights learned from previous sections, one can continue to practice having quality discussions. In preparation,

- Choose an appropriate setting for the discussion.
- Listen to each other's stories as they pertain to the question.
- Ask clarifying questions.
- Verbalize appreciation for the time together.
- Agree on the rules of engagement. For example,
    - Avoid name-calling or crosstalk.
    - Adhere to a two-minute time limit when sharing an opinion.
    - No changing topics mid-discussion.

- 🎤 The liberties of the healthy are being restricted during COVID-19 and is unconstitutional.

- 🎤 Those most responsible for correcting white privilege in our country are white people.

- 🎤 No matter the cause, tolerating vandalism to avoid confrontation sets a dangerous precedent and attracts further destruction.

- 🎤 It is acceptable for a business owner to refuse services to a customer based on religious convictions.

- 🎤 It is appropriate for public companies to boycott a state with strict abortion laws.

- 🎤 Transgendered individuals who undergo reassignment therapy should not be able to participate in competitive sporting events.

- 🎤 Mental health screenings on a regular basis should be a federal mandate for gun owners.

- 🎤 Homelessness is the failure of local politicians who are too lenient on drugs and loitering.

- 🎤 The culture within an ethnic group is the greatest factor impacting the quality of life for those feeling marginalized.

- 🎤 The creation of no-go zones for police and city officials sows the seeds of anarchy and should be eliminated or deterred.

- 🎤 A single-payer system is needed to reform our healthcare, as those most vulnerable continue to be ignored by our fraudulent health insurance policies.

- 🎤 Factions are using marginalized populations to destabilize the security of our nation for their own agenda.

- 🎤 The newest marginalized group is people of faith being shamed or killed for their convictions.

- 🎤 The LGBTQ community is always vulnerable where unjust laws are passed or just laws repealed.

- 🎤 Immigration laws in our country continue to be unjust and reflect an imperialistic society.

- 🎤 Black history is not the same as American history.

- As private entities, social media platforms have the right to censor content as they deem necessary.

- Our cancel culture reflects misplaced anger more than acts of justice.

- The state is too involved with public education and is not allowing teachers to meet the needs of the classroom as they deem necessary.

- Media should be liable for damages to an individual if they have intentionally exaggerated a story for their own narrative.

- As a deterrent, police should personally pay for any damage they incur while enforcing the law.

- Our society is making decisions out of fear instead of reason leading to destructive policies.

- The most fundamental injustices in our country are not related to race, sex, or religion but to the growing divide between our socioeconomic classes.

- State officials have the authority to enforce public order, and federal officers should not intervene.

ABOUT THE AUTHOR

Since the 2016 elections in the United States, Mark Fosdal has either moderated or participated in discussions with a variety of organizations, including Make America Dinner Again, Living Room Conversations, Braver Angels, and 3Practices. Each organization had the shared goal of creating understanding between individuals having different political ideologies. His approach to moderating political discussions was highlighted by Anika Gupta in *How to Handle a Crowd*.

Over time, he created pearls of wisdom or insights in response to trends he observed with people's genuine struggle when conversing with others as well as insights addressing principle differences between ideologies. By empowering others to identify how their story is linked to their bias and temperament, Fosdal is striving to facilitate an environment that sustains quality discussions in order to build stronger relationships.

Originally from Wisconsin, he now lives in the greater Seattle area enjoying the outdoors of the Pacific Northwest. He applies the disciplined approach of critical thinking established during his career in cancer research to creating productive discussions to achieve a common goal of mutual understanding and respect.

Remain curious while knowing your life's story is the essence of civil dialogue.

Milton Keynes UK
Ingram Content Group UK Ltd.
UKHW050756250224
438379UK00012B/1258